OREGON
LAND OF MANY DREAMS

Text by
Suzi Forbes

CRESCENT BOOKS
NEW YORK

CLB 1542
© 1988 Colour Library Books Ltd., Guildford, Surrey, England.
All rights reserved.
Printed and bound in Barcelona, Spain by Cronion, S.A.
Published 1988 by Crescent Books, distributed by Crown Publishers, Inc.
ISBN 0 517 61055 8
h g f e d c b a

Oregon. The very word spells romance and beauty. From craggy, snow-topped peaks to rushing rivers. From expansive, sandy beaches to sheer cliffs that plummet into the Pacific Ocean. From sky-blue, crystal-clear lakes to gently-flowing streams, Oregon has a grandeur unmatched by other states.

Oregon is a land of contrasts and of contentment. It's an abrupt land, where waves crash against the shore, creating jagged cliffs and rocky promontories; where cliffs surge out of the sea onto flat mesas that give way in turn to valleys and hills. The mountains are always there in the background, like the backdrop to a stage set. Rushing rivers create fertile valleys. It's a land of abundance. And it's not called "God's Country" for nothing.

The Cascade Mountains create a wall dividing the lush, green valleys of the coastal area, blessed by warm rains, from the arid, hot and dry land on the east. There, a perpetual drought creates a stunted land of juniper and sagebrush.

History indicates that as early as 1542 the Portuguese explorer Juan Rodriguez Cabrillo, or at least his pilot Bartolome Ferrelo, may have been the first white men to set eyes on Oregon. If so, they were undoubtedly looking for that elusive waterway that mythology told them would lead directly to cities of gold and gems. Cabrillo was unsuccessful, and the Spanish/Portuguese dominance of the seas was coming to an end. But Great Britain was not far behind.

Sir Francis Drake followed on Cabrillo's heels in 1579. Whether he actually reached the Oregon Coast in his run north from California is unclear. If he did, he left no trace. It would be another 200 years before Oregon was actually "discovered." During that period, an entire nation would rise on the Eastern Coast, proclaim its independence from Great Britain, win a war solidifying that independence and gain international stature and prestige.

In that intervening time Indians inhabited Oregon. They lived a peaceful, tranquil life, fishing from the streams and eating berries and roots. There were twelve distinct families in all.

The Chinookans, of which the Clatsops and Cathlamets were major tribes, lived along the south shore of the Columbia. The Clackamas family lived in the Clackamas Valley and near Willamette Falls, while the Athapascans were on the Clatskanie and Nehalem Rivers. They were said to be so warlike that Hudson's Bay trappers learned not to traverse their territory unless they were at least 60 strong.

The Umpquas and the Siuslaws formed one family who lived in the southwest. Then there were the Salishans, the Yakonians and the Kusans, generally spread out along the coast. The Willamette Valley was occupied by the powerful Kalapooyans, who achieved a distinctive character by flattening their heads. The Tualati possessed the Tualatin River, while the Sahaptians, the Takelmans and the Hokans had control of the southern and eastern part of Oregon.

Actually, the Sahaptians were family to some of the best known tribes in history – the Nez Perce, the Umatillah, the Snake and the Cayuse. The Cayuse, in particular, had undergone a distinct change about 25 years before white men started visiting in numbers. The introduction of horses had turned them from a stable, peace-loving tribe into a warlike, nomadic one. Their freedom to move easily and quickly put them in a class by themselves. They were feared by Indian and white man alike.

Indian legends account for many of the natural wonders of Oregon. There's the story of Loowit, for example, a beautiful Indian girl, who was loved by two rivals. Loowit lived on Bridge of the Gods, which once spanned the Columbia River at the Cascades. As the rivalry intensified between her two lovers, a happy settlement became impossible. Therefore, the Gods turned Loowit into Mount St. Helens, while her two lovers became Mount Adams and Mount Hood. Loowit is still arguing against this injustice.

The white man has his legends too. It's Paul Bunyan and his great blue ox, Babe, who are credited by many for the creation of Spencer's Butte, the Columbia River and Crater Lake. It's said that the Columbia was created one day when Babe was feeling ornery and broke away from a plow. He made a headlong dash from the mountains to the sea, leaving a massive gash in the land behind. Paul was angry when he saw the damage Babe had done so he filled the gash with water.

It's said that Paul created Crater Lake when he found a huge reservoir of blue snow – the last of its kind. He dumped it into Crater Lake, where it turned that water into the lovely azure blue that has astonished travelers ever since.

Some folks, geologists in particular, have other explanations for these natural phenomena. It was probably as long as seventy-five million years ago that a barrier continuing from California to British Columbia started rising from the sea off the coast. This barrier eventually became the Sierra Nevada Range in California and the Cascade Range in Oregon and Washington. As the barrier rose, it shut out the sea from the interior and was responsible for creating a great drainage area, later to become the Columbia River. It turned the area to the west into a marine environment and that to the east into a drier one.

About fifty million years ago, eastern Oregon was dotted with lovely lakes. The Cascade hills were green with forests and beautiful with large, flowering shrubs. Magnolia, cinnamon and fig trees flourished and sycamore, dogwood and oak appeared. The Oregon grape, not the state flower, grew densely in the hills. Sequoia trees towered to imposing heights.

This was the era of giant mammals, as well. Dr. Thomas Condon, Oregon's famed pioneer geologist, discovered giant fossil beds in eastern Oregon in 1862. It is now certain that, over the past 50 million years, camels roamed the area, along with saber-toothed cats, mastodons, mammoths, giant mylodons – a sloth as large as a grizzly bear – elephants, horses and many smaller animals.

This era was followed by an age of volcanic activity. As mountains all along the Cascade Mountain Range belched smoke and lava, their residue filled in the blue lakes of eastern Oregon. It was during this period that Oregon's coast extended well into the Pacific Ocean. Following this great upheaval, however, the coastal land went through a period of depression. Land that then formed the coastline is now submerged well out into the ocean.

Further volcanic activity followed, creating the magnificent peaks of Mount Hood, Mount Jefferson, the Three Sisters and the largest of them all, the sky-piercing Mount Mazama. It is believed that Mount Mazama at one time exceeded 14,000 feet and was the highest peak in the Cascade Mountain Range.

The ice age followed, although it appears that Oregon was never totally engulfed in ice during this period. One of the few remnants of the ice age in Oregon is Wallowa Lake in northeastern Oregon. It is a glacial lake six miles long, one-quarter mile wide and between six and seven hundred feet deep.

It was at the end of the ice age, as recently as 7,000 years ago, that one of the great wonders of nature occurred. Grand Mount Mazama probably suffered a massive volcanic explosion, which is said to have been so tremendous that ash covered the entire Northwestern United States, reaching as far as Saskatchewan, Canada. The result was the creation of Crater Lake. Unlike most lakes which are fed or drained by rivers or streams, Crater Lake has no natural outlet. Over the years, precipitation and seepage have been perfectly balanced by evaporation to create this clean, blue lake six miles in diameter and over 2,000 feet deep. It is now a national park.

Another period of land depression followed when the coast slipped away a bit more and the Willamette Valley became a fresh-water lake caused by the damming of the Columbia by ice. At that time, the Willamette River flowed 300 feet above the present level of Portland.

Gradually, the Willamette Valley lake receded, and today we are experiencing renewed volcanic activity. Mount Hood erupted in 1865 and Mount St. Helens in 1843, 1980 and 1985.

Traces of early human inhabitants in Oregon are numerous. Cave and canyon pictures have been found near The Dalles, Arlington and Forest Grove as well as in other, more remote, areas.

It's Captain James Cook whom we credit with the European discovery of Oregon. One day in 1778 Cook skittered northward from the South Pacific where he had languished in the sun for eighteen months. On his way north, he found the Sandwich Islands (Hawaii) and then reached the Oregon Coast in March. Sailing ever northward, he landed in Nootka Sound on present-day Vancouver Island, where friendly Indians offered him furs.

Still traveling north, Cook eventually sailed through the Bering Strait separating Alaska from Russia. He called it "the western extremity of all America." Cook then returned to the Sandwich Islands, where he infuriated the native Hawaiians by chopping up a temple to provide firewood for his ship. Cook's sailing days were over. The Hawaiians killed him for his sacrilege.

But Cook's men continued on to China – Canton to be exact – to sell their wares. Much to their surprise, they found the furs to be their most popular item. "Skins which did not cost the purchaser sixpence sterling," wrote one man, "sold for one hundred dollars." That did it. They couldn't wait to return to Oregon to pick up another load.

In no time at all, ships from England, Portugal, Spain, France and even the fledgling American Republic were flying back and forth with their precious cargoes of furs – especially the highly-prized otter skins.

Because the fur trade was increasing in importance, countries sent their best explorers to research it. Great Britain, for example, sent Captain George Vancouver, who spent the better part of three summers exploring inlets, sounds and rivers from San Diego in California to Cook's Inlet in Alaska – always searching for the Northwest Passage. In the process, he charted the California, Oregon, Washington and British Columbia coasts.

Fur traders learned they could get the best prices from Indians who had never seen a white man. This led to more innovative explorations in remote, isolated areas. Finally, in May, 1792, Captain Robert Gray frisked across the breakers into the mouth of a giant river. He traveled about thirty miles inland, trading with the Indians along the way. He named the mighty river after his ship the *Columbia*.

Gray was an American, and his voyage opened new horizons for a new country that had only recently won its freedom from Great Britain. Gray's ship had been fitted out and financed in Boston. On his first trip he collected over 700 otter skins on the Pacific Coast and then sold them in China. It seems that men thrilled to the sight of these lovely silver furs tipped with white and would pay almost anything for them.

When Gray returned to Boston from his second voyage, he brought a handsome profit for his backers. In fact, it is reputed the *Columbia* did so well that by 1804 there were over fifty ships occupied in the "China Trade" from Boston to the Northwest, to the Sandwich Islands, and then to China and back to Boston. During the years 1801-1802 more than 15,000 sea otter skins were collected. Profit on one voyage alone was $90,000 and on another, $234,000. Not bad for two years work in the early 19th Century!

Meanwhile, even though Daniel Boone had led his band of settlers into Kentucky's wilderness in 1769, there seemed to be no reason to push further west. In fact, it wasn't until 1793 that Alexander Mackenzie started thinking about an overland route to the Pacific. Maybe that was the way to find the elusive Northwest Passage.

Mackenzie was a Canadian with an interest in a small rival to the mighty Hudson's Bay Company, called the North West Company. He knew that if he could establish a land route to the abundant furs of the Northwest before Hudson's Bay could, he would have a profitable venture. Mackenzie set out with ten woodsmen and an ample store of provisions. He became the first man to traverse the entire North American continent. Even though a direct route to the mighty river that Gray described had eluded him, his adventure sparked the imaginations of other industrious men.

Among them was Thomas Jefferson, who had become the third President of the United States in 1801. He was restless to learn everything possible about this great nation he had helped to found. He admitted that "the works of nature in the large" were especially fascinating to him and he longed to learn more about the mountains, rivers and geographic masses of his continent.

And so, in January 1803, Jefferson sent a message to Congress recommending an exploring expedition to the Pacific. He said: "An intelligent officer, with ten or twelve men fit for the enterprise, and willing to undertake it, might explore the whole line, even to the Western Ocean, have conferences with the natives on the subject of commercial intercourse, get admission among them for our traders, as others are admitted, agree on a convenient deposit for an interchange of articles, and return with the information acquired in the course of two summers."

Meriwether Lewis, then twenty-nine years old, was secretary to President Jefferson. It seems he had known Jefferson for some time, having been raised near the president's home at Monticello in Virginia. He asked if he might lead the expedition. Jefferson agreed.

Lewis had always wanted to see the great untamed West. He seems outwardly to have been an unlikely candidate – a shy, moody man, even awkward. Yet he found that the challenge of nature met his innermost needs.

He had always loved to hunt, and was a supreme woodsman. Furthermore, he had been in the regular army and was familiar with the discipline required of such an expedition. Jefferson said of Lewis, that he was "Honest, disinterested, of sound understanding, and fidelity to truth so scrupulous that whatever he should report would be as certain as if seen by ourselves." He also observed that he was "steady in the maintenance of discipline" and would be "careful as a father of those committed to his charge."

Lewis chose William Clark as his partner. Clark, unlike

Lewis, was an outgoing, friendly, affable man who seems to have understood nature on its own terms. A practical man, he was up to any challenge of man or nature.

Clark was a military man as well. He had traveled in the West, first participating in the campaign against the Ohio Indians and then exploring on his own, even crossing the Mississippi River several times.

Jefferson's instructions were to "explore the Missouri River and such principal stream of it as, by its course and communication with the waters of the Pacific Ocean, whether the Columbia, Oregon, Colorado or some other river, may offer the most direct and practical water communication across the continent for the purpose of commerce." They were still looking for that elusive Northwest Passage.

The president insisted on strict record-keeping, and instructed them to note everything – from birds, flowers and wildlife to the important locations of rivers and mountains. He even suggested they make several copies of their notes to guard against the only record being lost to the elements. He urged all the men to keep individual diaries of their personal observations, and some did.

As to the Indians they would encounter, Jefferson instructed the explorers to "treat them in the most friendly and conciliatory manner which their own conduct will admit." He even suggested they might want to arrange to have several influential chiefs visit Washington.

Finally, Jefferson's instructions about their own safety say much for the great man. He said, "We wish you to err on the side of your safety, and to bring back your party safe, even if it be with less information."

On May 14, 1804, a party of twenty-three set out from St. Louis, then an outpost frontier and the center of the fur trade. Lewis brought his dog and Clark brought his slave. He turned out to be the first black man, and also the largest, ever seen by the Indians, and he caused quite a stir wherever he went. Finally, they added a fiddle for song and laughter around the campfire.

The men accompanying Lewis and Clark were military men, too – a shrewd move on Jefferson's part, because this meant the military paid their salaries. They were lean and tough and used to a rough but disciplined life.

On May 25th, they passed La Charette, the home of Daniel Boone and the last settlement on the Missouri. From here on it was open space. As they traveled, they found buffalo roaming in great herds. It was buffalo stew that fed the hungry men around the campfire at night.

It took them five months to reach their winter camp near present-day Bismarck, North Dakota. A lucky discovery, however, resulted in an addition to their expedition that made the rest of the trip more fun and less dangerous.

A middle-aged French-Canadian named Charbonneau knew the language of several Indian tribes they would encounter along the way. They asked him to join their expedition as interpreter. His seventeen-year-old wife, Sacagawea, was familiar with the land they would be crossing. She was a Shoshone princess, who had been kidnapped four years earlier and even knew of "the pass through the mountains." Before the band moved on in April, 1805, Sacagawea had given birth to a baby boy, who became the darling of the camp.

Soon they were passing through vast plains near the mouth of the Yellowstone. They wrote they were "animated by vast herds of buffalo, deer, elk and antelope." The animals were so friendly they "often followed quietly for some distance."

The grizzly bears certainly exhibited no fear of the explorers. Indeed, on one occasion, Captain Lewis turned around to find a snarling beast rushing pell-mell toward him. He raced for the river bank, jumped in and somehow missed being torn to pieces.

On they pressed through fields and mountains, fording streams and traveling by river. Finally, they reached the land of the Shoshone Indians.

No one was happier than Sacagawea. She began to dance "and show every mark of the most extravagant joy..." Not only had she found her people again, but it turned out the chief was her brother. The Shoshone were pleased to help. They provided horses and guides through the treacherous mountain pass. Without them, Lewis and Clark might not have been able to complete their journey.

They climbed mountains higher than they had ever imagined, sometimes with sheer, rocky faces, and passed through forests so dense they couldn't see one another. They built canoes to carry them down the rivers, passing from the Salmon to the Snake and then to the Columbia that Gray had earlier explored from its mouth. On November 15, 1805, Lewis, Clark and their entourage saw the peaceful waves of the Pacific Ocean lapping against the sandy shore. They had traversed a continent!

They recorded their impressions of the valley which extended "a great distance to the right and left, rich thickly covered with tall timber, with a fiew Small Praries bordering on the river and on the Islands; Some fiew standing Ponds and Several Small Streams of running water on either Side of the river. This is certainly a fertill and handsome valley, at this time crouded with Indians."

They spent the winter on the coast near present-day Seaside, Oregon – naming the outpost Fort Clatsop. All winter it rained. They erected shelters to protect themselves from the cold and wet, but these were inadequate. Food was perilously low. On Christmas Day 1805, Captain Clark wrote; "Some rain at different times last night and showers of hail with intervals of fair starr light... The day proved showery all day... Our Store of meat entirely Spoiled... Our Dinner to day consisted of poor Elk boiled, spoiled fish and some roots."

They made the return trip in the spring of 1806, reaching St. Louis again on September 23, 1806. They were lucky. During the entire two and one-half year expedition, they lost only one man, and that was probably due to appendicitis.

A grateful President Jefferson and Congress gave both Lewis and Clark 1,600 acres of land and generously rewarded the rest of the men with 320 acres and doubled their pay.

Why all this interest in establishing a route to the Pacific Ocean? Jefferson's interest in nature and knowledge undoubtedly played a role. On the other hand, he was a shrewd politician and an ardent pacifist who realized that by laying claim to these vast territories before someone else did, he could preserve them for the United States. And anyway, he had just arranged the Louisiana Purchase, which included all the land to present-day Idaho on the north and to Texas on the south. He visualized whole new territories opening up for commerce, especially in the fur trade.

Meanwhile, there was much speculation about the new land that had just been explored. Jefferson himself asked a traveler to the west to check out a report that "The Lama or Paca of Peru is found in those part of this continent..."

Men had sought the Northwest Passage for so long it was difficult to set aside the myth of a great river that flowed east to west. They even had a name for it – The Oregon River. These myths died a hard death, even after Lewis and Clark returned. Somewhere out there the "River of the West" must lead directly to the Pacific. Men continued their search.

The race for trade dominance of the Oregon Country, as it was called, intensified. The North West Company, stimulated by news of the Lewis and Clark expedition, established a trading post in the Rocky Mountains.

In 1807, Simon Fraser descended the river that bears his name and founded a post where it empties into Puget Sound near present-day Vancouver, British Columbia. His disappointment was intense when he realized he had fallen into the same trap as Alexander Mackenzie in 1793. The river he thought was the Columbia was actually several hundred miles north of that mighty river. The North West Company, straining every effort to stave off an American occupation, pressed on.

However, enterprise was equally creative in the United States. John Jacob Astor had watched the Lewis and Clark expedition with special interest. Astor had been engaged in the fur trade for several years, and he knew that at least seventy-five percent of the furs that entered the United States came from Canada.

He operated a fleet of ships out of New York to China. It galled him to buy his furs from such companies as the North West Company and Hudson's Bay Company in Canada. So, in 1808, he secured a charter from President Jefferson and organized a new company to operate out of New York. He called it the Pacific Fur Company.

Astor outfitted an overland party and, as custom demanded, they set out on their adventure from St. Louis. They followed a route that would later become the Oregon Trail, arriving at the mouth of the Columbia River in January 1812.

Astor had sent another contingent of men via a sea route and they arrived ahead of the overland party. Their voyage had been beset by problems, however. Sickness, bickering and an Indian massacre had left the ship in ruins and a mere five sailors to greet the overlanders.

It was an ominous start for Astor's Pacific Fur Trading Company. Left alone in this abandoned outpost they called "Astoria," the men became discouraged and depressed. Finally, in May 1812, the supply ship *Beaver* showed up bringing nails, liquor, food, clothing and fresh courage.

Men and supplies continued to arrive, and the little trading post called Astoria flourished. But, alas, not for long. When news reached Astoria in 1813 that the United States was at war with Great Britain again, Astorians feared the worst. The North West Company was able to convince the British that their interests in the Pacific region must be secured. The British Admiralty promised to send naval support. Neither the United States government nor Astor were able to defend their claim. When news came that a British man-of-war would be arriving shortly, plans were made to sell Astoria – fur, supplies, fort and all.

The North West Company was eager to buy. Why wait for the British man-of-war and allow the fort to become the property of the British government? They bought the outpost for $58,291. Thus ended John Jacob Astor's association with the fur trade in the Pacific Northwest.

Even the name Astoria was used no more. The North West Company renamed the outpost Fort George. The abandonment of the fort in Astoria by the Americans left all the fur trade routes to the British. Keen competition developed between the Hudson's Bay Company and the North West Company. Indeed, so keen was the competition that agents of both companies resorted to ambush, arson, thievery, kidnapping and even murder to further their own interests. Folks as far away as London were concerned. Finally, in 1821, a merger was negotiated between the two great companies. The name Hudson's Bay Company was retained. After all, hadn't they always imperiously claimed their initials stood for "Here Before Christ?" The North West Company was no more.

With the merger came renewed interest in establishing secure fur routes, interspersed with trading posts all along the Oregon Trail, connecting with the trading posts already established across Canada, and culminating at the mouth of the Columbia, where ships would transport the goods to China. Haste was essential. Now that the war with the United States was over, Americans were showing renewed interest in a cross-country fur route.

Oregon history abounds with descriptions of the men who crossed this frontier. There was Dr. John McLaughlin, named by the Hudson's Bay Company as Chief Factor for the Columbia District. He had been a physician to the North West Company and is described as six feet four inches tall, with piercing eyes and a strong, raw-boned appearance.

We have the following description by George Simpson, governor of the Northern Department and Columbia District, when they met by chance on the trail: "such a figure as I should not like to meet in a dark Night in one of the bye lanes in the neighborhood of London... He was dressed in Clothes that had once been fashionable, but now covered with a thousand patches of different Colors, his beard would do honor to the chin of a Grizzley Bear, his face and hands evidently Shewing up that he had not lost much time at his Toilette, loaded with Arms and his own herculean dimensions forming a tout ensemble that would convey a good idea of the highway men of former Days."

George Simpson himself was an interesting character. He was born in Scotland, but employment in a London mercantile firm brought him to the attention of the Hudson's Bay Company. He was brilliant and climbed rapidly up the ladder of success. The official Hudson's Bay Company history says of him: "He had the imaginative vision of a Clive; he drew his plans on a scale that was continental" and "In him a clear orderly mind and a driving ambition were sustained by a physical vitality which carried him bouyantly through life." He was eventually knighted by the British sovereign for his accomplishments.

After meeting on the trail to Oregon, Simpson and McLaughlin continued to Fort George (Astoria) together. They made preparations to redesign completely their Pacific Coast operations. They began by moving the headquarters post to a point on the north side of the Columbia River, opposite present-day Portland. They were certain, no matter what, that the territory north of the Columbia would always remain in British hands. They named their new post Fort Vancouver, after the great explorer.

By March 15, 1825, the new fort was complete and Simpson dedicated it. He recounted the day in his journal: "At Sun rise mustered all the people to hoist the Flag Staff of the new Establishment and in presence of the Gentlemen, Servants, Chiefs and Indians, I Baptised it by breaking a Bottle of Rum on the Flag Staff and repeating the following words in a loud voice, 'In behalf of the Hon. Hudson's Bay Company I hereby name this Establishment Fort Vancouver. God Save King George the Fourth.' with three cheers.... The object of naming it after that distinguished navigator is to identify our claim to the Soil and Trade with his discovery of the River and Coast on behalf of Great Britain."

The Hudson's Bay Company's Fort Vancouver was to grow continually in importance. McLaughlin was in charge and he encouraged new trades such as raising corn, peas, oats, barley and wheat in the rich river soil. It became the leading port city, where all goods from the inland were transported for shipment elsewhere and where supplies arrived. The fur trade grew in importance, along with Fort Vancouver's prosperity.

New settlers continued to arrive to swell Vancouver's population. Soon they established a carpenter shop, church, bake house, blacksmith shop, stables, a hospital and a flour mill. When the American Lieutenant Charles Wilkes visited Fort Vancouver in 1841, he wrote; "(It) is a large manufacturing, agricultural and commercial depot, and there are few if any idlers, except the sick. Everybody seems to be in a hurry, whilst there appears to be no obvious reason for it."

Dr. McLaughlin remained in charge of Fort Vancouver for twenty-two years and was known for his tolerant but firm attitude toward the Indians, his business expertise and his warm hospitality to American settlers, traders and missionaries. He was deservedly known as the "Father of Oregon."

He established a vigorous export trade, especially in wheat and flour. By 1846, for example, he exported 6,000 barrels of flour to Alaska. He built a sawmill near Fort Vancouver and produced and sold lumber. He even exported some to Hawaii and he established a vigorous trade in salmon.

Fort Vancouver seems to have had a pleasant social life as well, holding balls, regattas and dinners for the entertainment of its citizens. They ate good food at polished tables set with silver and Spode, read good books and engaged in stimulating conversation. The wives of the officers were generally bright and intelligent half-castes.

As good as life was, the fact that the Hudson's Bay Company was a monopoly, and without the benefit of competition, was bound to be a source of dissatisfaction. They set their own prices for the sale of goods from London, usually with a 100 percent markup. And they set a firm price for the purchase of goods from the settlers – not subject to negotiation.

The Americans had not been idle in their efforts to obtain an influential position in Oregon since the War of 1812. Actually, Astoria was restored to the American government in the Convention of 1818, but nothing came of it. At the same time, a treaty was signed between Great Britain and the United States granting joint occupation of the Oregon territory for ten years.

Oregon Territory now comprised an area that extended north to the 54°40' parallel and south to the 42nd; east to the Rocky Mountains and west to the Pacific Ocean. The Convention of 1818 also recognized the 49th parallel as the northern boundary of the United States as far west as the Rockies.

In 1823, Representative John Floyd of Virginia even had the foresight to introduce a bill in Congress that would recognize an American interest in Oregon Country. He spoke of the importance of the Columbia River to American commerce. It would provide a safe harbor for whalers traveling from New England. It would also serve as a base for an established fur trade in the United States and it would provide a port in the Pacific Northwest from which to carry on the China Trade. He also saw the territory as a place for eventual expansion. He could see settlers moving west to farm or open shops. But

all this was too much for Congress to comprehend in 1823. They defeated the bill.

Subsequent negotiations between Great Britain and the United States eventually narrowed the controversy over boundary. The United States contended that its territory should extend west to the Pacific Ocean along the 49th parallel. Great Britain thought the boundary should extend along the 49th parallel to the point where the Columbia River intersects it and then follow the line of the River south. Under this proposal, most of the current state of Washington would remain British. But great strides had been made to narrow the controversy to these positions.

Meanwhile, more and more settlers had been migrating to the Oregon Territory – almost all of them American. There were mountain men like Jedediah Smith, David Jackson and the Sublett brothers, William, Milton and Andrew, who set up trapping expeditions in the mountains and, as a sideline, sold supplies to other trappers, Indians and folks they ran into on the trail. Prices were high, but there was little choice. In 1826 scarlet cloth, for example, went for $6.00 a yard; beaver traps for $9.00 and firewater for $13.50 a gallon. "Outfitting" became more profitable than trapping.

Hall Kelley was a Boston schoolteacher who had read Lewis and Clark's account of the West. In 1829 he formed a society dedicated to settling the West. He called it the American Society for Encouraging the Settlement of the Oregon Territory. In typical Puritan fashion, he felt a planned settlement would provide refuge for the unfortunate, improve the moral character of the Indians and break Great Britain's hold on the West.

Kelley wrote many pamphlets and brochures promoting his enterprise and, although he had never been there himself, described the land in vivid phrases. "Much of the country within two hundred miles of the ocean, is favorable to cultivate," he wrote. "The valley of the Multnomah (Willamette) is extremely fertile... The Oregon is covered with heavy forests of timber... The production of vegetables, grain and cattle will require comparitively but little labor; these articles, together with the spontaneous growth of the soil, and the fruits of laborious industry, in general will find a market, at home, and thereby comfort and enrich the settlers. Surplus staple articles may be shipped from their doors to distant ports, and return a vast profit in trade."

Although Kelley's colonization efforts never materialized for him, his tracts stirred much interest. In fact, Nathaniel J. Wyeth thought it sounded as if the time was right to establish an American company that would rival the Hudson's Bay

Company. Accordingly, he organized the Pacific Trading Company.

He led an expedition to Oregon in 1832 that left St. Louis with twenty-four men. Sickness and disaster plagued them. They arrived at the gates of Fort Vancouver merely eleven strong. McLaughlin made it clear he would not tolerate a competitive fur trading company but Wyeth had no money anyway. Several of his men elected to remain in Oregon but a discouraged Wyeth went back to Boston, to return again in 1834. This expedition met a similar fate. He remained for two years only and returned to Boston – this time to stay. So much for an American rival to the Hudson's Bay Company.

John Townsend had accompanied Wyeth on his second expedition. As a chronicler, he gives us excellent insight into the character of the land. "Wheat thrives astonishingly; I never saw better in any country, and the various culinary vegetables... are in great profusion, and of the first quality." He also wrote about the Indians: "...In a very few years the race must, in the nature of things, become extinct; and the time is probably not far distant, when the little trinkets and toys of this people will be picked up... as mementoes of a nation passed away for ever from the face of the earth."

Jason Lee, a minister for the Methodist Ministry Society, his nephew Daniel Lee, also a minister, and their lay helpers Philip Edwards, Cyrus Shepard and Courtney M. Walker had joined the second Wyeth expedition to set up a mission among the Indians. After spending some time at Fort Vancouver, they searched for a likely spot. Lee's choice was a lovely location in the Willamette Valley, ten miles north of the present site of Salem, Oregon. He wrote it was "so situated as to form a central position from which missionary labors may be extended in almost every direction among the natives and those emigrants who may hereafter settle in that vast and fertile territory."

Lee immediately set about the task of building and organizing a school. A mere four years later he could boast to headquarters that he had admitted fifty-two Indian pupils to his school. His success so impressed the Mission Society they sent thirteen more men and women in 1836.

Feeling the need for even more reinforcements, Lee traveled east in 1838. He must have been a great orator and enthusiastic about his topic, for this time the congregations supplied him with $100,000, thirty-two adults, eighteen children and a ship to bring them all west. They brought enough goods to set up a mission store, as well as tools to build even more homes, churches, schools and mission stations.

Chief among their new stations was the one at The Dalles. In 1841 Jason Lee reportedly baptised over 130 individuals and gave the sacraments to 500 at The Dalles. That does not necessarily mean, however, that all those Indians were converted to Christianity.

Indeed, there is considerable evidence the Methodist missionaries and the Indians understood very little about one another. During an eruption of Mt. St. Helens, for example, in 1843, the Indians exhibited terror of a God who would command fire to shoot into the air and cause the earth to shake. The missionaries exalted such a God and impulsively broke into song. The Indians were totally bewildered. Missionary theology dealt with ideas while Indian religion dealt with outward exhibits of power. It was hard to reconcile the two.

As the difficulty of the task of converting the Indians to Christianity became more apparent, the interest in missionary work dwindled. The missionaries spent more and more of their time furthering the work of the settlement. They planted crops, increased their cattle herds and built even more houses, stables and stores. A visitor in 1841 noted, "As far as my personal observation went... they seem more occupied with the settlement of the country and in the agricultural pursuits than in the missionary labors."

Finally, in 1843, Lee was suspended from his post. He and his brother returned East. Their school was taken over in 1844 by the Oregon Institute and is now part of Willamette University. Nevertheless, many of the missionary band remained in the Willamette Valley as settlers. They eventually formed the nucleus that attracted so many future settlers to this lush land.

The coastal region and the Willamette Valley weren't the only places that attracted missionaries. In 1835 the American Board of Commissioners for Foreign Missions sent out Dr. Samuel Parker to see if they should set up missions in Oregon Territory. He was accompanied by young Dr. Marcus Whitman. They found lots of Indians to convert so, without even going the full distance to Fort Vancouver, Whitman returned east to bring out supplies and more assistants. He married his childhood sweetheart and brought her along. Reverend and Mrs. Henry Narman Spalding volunteered to come as well. These two women, except for Sacagawea, proved to be the first women to make the overland trip.

In order to carry even more supplies, they took wagons – later even converting one to a cart. Thus they were the first expedition to take a wagon as far as Fort Boise. It was only a matter of time before wagons would make the journey all the way to the Pacific Ocean. Six months after arriving at Fort Vancouver, Narcissa Whitman gave birth to the first white child born west of the Continental Divide.

Dr. Parker had been busy while Dr. Whitman was in the East. He had staked out a number of sites for his missions. He assigned the Whitmans to one on the Walla Walla River, about twenty miles from the Columbia. Dr. Parker noted, "A mission located on this fertile field would draw around it an interesting settlement, who would fix down to cultivate the soil and to be instructed. How easily might the plough go through these vallies, and what rich and abundant harvests might be gathered by the hand of industry."

And that's exactly what the Whitmans did. They planted fields of grain and corn and taught the Indians to do the same. The Nez Perce Indians were intelligent and industrious and they learned quickly. The Cayuse Indians were less so and kept their distance – even exhibiting hostility at times.

Catholic missionaries came too. In 1838 Father Francis N. Blanchet, of the Montreal Diocese, arrived after an arduous journey of 5,325 miles from Montreal – a trip that had lasted six months. The Catholics set up missions on the Cowlitz River and near present-day Oregon City on the Willamette.

Cordial relations did not exist between the Catholics and the Protestants, to say the least. Had they ever? The British at Fort Vancouver and at other Hudson's Bay Company trading posts were mostly French Canadian Catholics. They encouraged the Catholic priests. Competition between the two factions was keen. Father Blanchet extended his missions and was soon elevated to Bishop.

It was clear to most everyone by now that the fur trade was diminishing. Beaver that had once been plentiful were now scarce. Otter no longer abounded. Even McLaughlin, who still ran Fort Vancouver for the Hudson's Bay Company, wrote as early as 1846, "Every One Knows who is acquainted with the Fur trade that as the country becomes settled the Fur trade Must Diminish."

Several events took place that spurred a new interest in the settlement of the Oregon Country. In 1836 the immensely popular novelist, Washington Irving, had written a two-volume work called *Astoria*. It was widely read. And that was only the beginning. Newspapers began to romanticize the West.

Westward Ho!! By 1843 "Oregon Fever" had set in. That was the year of the Great Migration. It was the year 875 new emigrants settled the Willamette Valley; the year the first

covered wagons made it as far as The Dalles and the year seven hundred head of cattle were driven over the Oregon Trail.

In 1839 the population of the Willamette Valley was estimated at 100 souls. By 1843 the number had swollen to one thousand five hundred – and all except sixty-one were American. Huge caravans now started the westward trek. By 1845 the population of the territory had grown to 6,000.

It's hard for us to imagine today the rigors and hardships of cross-country travel by wagon train. It was imperative that strict discipline and time schedules be maintained. The trains usually left St. Louis by mid-May, when the rivers had receded enough to ford and the grass was sufficient for the livestock. Our best accounts are from journals kept by the travelers themselves.

Jesse Applegate came in the Great Migration of 1843. He became a leader in Oregon and later wrote of his cross-country adventures:

"It is four o'clock am; the sentinels on duty have discharged their rifles – the signal that the hours of sleep are over – and every wagon and tent is pouring forth its night's tenants, and slowly kindling smokes begin largely to rise and float away in the morning air... breakfast is to be eaten, the tents struck, the wagons loaded and the teams yoked and brought up in readiness to be attached to their respective wagons. All know when, at seven o'clock the signal to march sounds, that those not ready to take their proper places in the line of march must fall into the dusty rear for the day...

"The sun is now getting low in the west, and at length the painstaking pilot is standing ready to conduct the train in the circle which he has previously measured and marked out, which is to form the invariable fortification for the night... Within ten minutes from the time the leading wagon halted, the barricade is formed, the teams unyoked and driven out to pasture. Everyone is busy preparing fires... to cook the evening meal, pitching tents and otherwise preparing for the night... The watches begin at eight o'clock pm. and end at four o'clock am."

Credit for the Great Migration has often been given to Dr. Whitman, but that is probably more myth than fact. It is true that in 1842 Whitman received a letter from the American Board advising him it had decided to close his mission. Not *his* mission! He immediately returned East by horseback to argue his case.

He traveled to New York, Washington and Boston,

convincing all he spoke to that a practical route and safe passage to Oregon could be assured by continuation of the missions. It has been suggested he also convinced folks of the need to save Oregon from the British.

Whitman even had an interview with that famous newspaperman, Horace Greeley, editor of the *New York Tribune*, but he didn't convince this doubting Thomas. Greeley would later pen the statement that has been paraphrased as "Go West, Young Man, Go West," but in 1843 he wrote:

"This emigration of more than a thousand persons in one body to Oregon wears an aspect of insanity. For what do they brave the desert, the wilderness, the savage, the snowy precipices of the Rocky Mountain, the weary summer march, the stormdrenched bivouac and the gnawings of famine?" When he said "Go West" he meant Chicago. Perhaps St. Louis or even Ohio, but never Oregon – that was insanity!

Be that as it may, with this new influx of emigrants from the United States there was more and more dissatisfaction with British rule. In 1843 some of the Americans in the Willamette Valley got together to draw up a provisional constitution – much as their ancestors had done less than one hundred years earlier in Philadelphia. They included a bill of rights with provisions requiring fairness to Indians and prohibiting slavery. It even included an innovative new method for filing land claims.

The cry for independence from Britain was joined by the rest of the nation, especially those in the Mississippi Valley. The United States was officially still offering to settle at the 49th parallel, but the nation wanted the territory north to the 54° 40' parallel. The cry of "54-40 or fight!" was chanted in legislatures and in the streets.

So intense was the nation's desire to annex Oregon they elected a president in 1844 who was committed to the cause, James Knox Polk. This president knew what he wanted: tariff reductions, California, treasury reform and settlement of the Oregon boundary question. He intended to be a one-term president, so he was in a hurry.

In Polk's inaugural address he boldly claimed all the Oregon territory north to 54°40'. To prove how reasonable he was, though, he offered to settle with Britain at the 49th a few days later. Britain refused. Polk publicly went back to the 54°40' position and proclaimed the United States would accept nothing less.

Loud protestations on both sides continued through all of

1845. But when, in 1846, the British offered to settle at 49 at least as far as the Puget Sound and then mid-channel through the Strait of Juan de Fuca to the Pacific, Polk demurred. He refused to commit himself but deferred to the Senate for "advice and consent." They quickly gave it and the treaty was signed on June 15, 1846.

It was characteristic of the great John McLaughlin, still Chief Factor of the Hudson's Bay Company, that he was one of the first to sign the oath of loyalty to the new provincial government. Throughout the years he had remained kind to the Indians, and welcomed American settlers, often providing them with money and food from his own storehouse and caring for their sick himself.

How was he remembered? The British attacked him as a traitor. He wrote: "Why? Because I acted as a Christian, saved American citizens, men, women and children from the Indian tomahawk and enabled them to take farms to support their families...?"

The Americans distrusted McLaughlin. He was British and Catholic! They eventually confiscated all his property. Ten years later as an old and sick man he wrote a plea to a young Oregon politician: "I might better have been shot forty years ago than to have lived here and tried to build up a family and an estate in this government. I became a citizen of the United States in good faith. I planted all I had here, and the government confiscated my property. Now what I want to ask of you is that you will give your influence after I am dead to have this property go to my children. I have earned it as other settlers have earned theirs, and it ought to be mine and my heirs." His lands were eventually restored to his heirs, but the "Father of Oregon" died penniless and disillusioned in 1857.

Things were not all that rosy for the Whitmans near Walla Walla either. Wagon trains made their mission a regular stop on the way west, but when the emigrant train of 1847 arrived, many children were sick with the measles. Soon the disease spread to the Indians, who had no built-up immunity. The white children recovered but the Indians died. The Indians took this as a sign Dr. Whitman was giving special attention to the whites and not enough to them. They even wondered if maybe he was giving them poison.

On October 29, 1847, the Cayuse Indians swooped down on the hapless mission. They scalped and slaughtered Dr. Whitman, Narcissa and many others unlucky enough to be present. Of the seventy-two people in the mission, the Indians killed fourteen and they took many hostages.

The Whitman Massacre raised strong feelings that Congress should declare the Oregon Country a territory of the United States. They sent a message to Washington, "Our relations with the proud and powerful tribes of Indians residing east of the Cascade Mountains, hitherto uniformly amicable and pacific, have recently assumed quite a different character. They have shouted the war whoop and crimsoned their tomahawks in the blood of our citizens... To repel the attacks of so formidable a foe, and protect our families and property from violence and rapine, will require more strength than we possess... we have the right to expect your aid, and you are in justice bound to extend it..."

Finally, in 1848, Congress created territorial status for Oregon Country. President Polk lost no time in appointing General Joseph Lane the first Territorial Governor of Oregon. Mountain man Joe Meek, who had sped to Washington with the terrible news of the Whitman Massacre and the subsequent Cayuse Wars, was appropriately named U.S. Marshal to the new Territory.

Lane and Meek immediately headed West. Because of the approach of winter they took the Southern route, arriving in San Francisco just as the California Gold Rush fever struck. They sailed by ship to the Columbia River, by canoe up the Columbia and finally up the Willamette River to Oregon City, site of the first territorial government. Ironically, news that Congress had created the Oregon Territory reached the outpost via the Hawaiian Islands, merely a month before Lane himself.

Oregon City was quite the metropolis by then. Its location on the Willamette Falls made it ideal for harnessing energy to power mills. It boasted the first newspaper, the *Oregon Spectator*, a population of 500, two blacksmiths, four tailors, two churches, two saloons, two hatters, two silversmiths, a tannery, two sawmills, two grist mills, a cooper, a cabinet maker and about seventy-five houses. In fact, the town had been founded by Dr. John McLaughlin when he retired from the Hudson's Bay Company in 1846. It was his land in Oregon City, and ownership of the Imperial Mills which he founded, that were later confiscated by the new government.

There was plenty for a new governor to do, that's for sure. To begin with, those Cayuse Indians continued to be very troublesome. The massacre of the Whitmans was only the beginning. Although some Cayuse had attempted to surrender, return the captives, apologize for the massacre and call the whole thing off, others were more belligerent. Oregon residents felt strongly that the murderers should be apprehended and punished. Sporadic fighting occurred throughout 1848.

On Governor Lane's arrival, preparations were immediately made for a fresh attack. The Cayuse knew these reinforcements were formidable. They offered to negotiate again. They would surrender the murderers in exchange for peace. Lane agreed. The five Indian warriors were handed over to federal officers in The Dalles. They were taken to Oregon City, tried, convicted of murder and hanged in 1850. Three years of Indian wars were finally over. Governor Lane's swift and decisive treatment of the Cayuse Indians set the tone for settling future disagreements with the Indians and was the example followed by subsequent Governors.

The Indian Wars didn't hinder growth in the region one bit, though. By 1857 records show that Oregon had 60,000 inhabitants in its rich farming valleys and towns. They were, indeed, becoming quite sophisticated. In that year alone, they shipped 60,000 barrels of flour, 3,000,000 pounds of bacon and pork, 250,000 pounds of butter, 25,000 bushels of apples, $40,000 worth of chickens and eggs, $200,000 worth of lumber, $75,000 worth of fruit trees and 52,000 head of cattle. The total value of all these exports amounted to $3,200,000. Not bad for a territory that hadn't even been granted statehood.

And Oregonians did feel it was time to push for statehood. The biggest question in Congress was whether to admit Oregon as a 'slave' or 'non-slave' state. No one in tough Oregon territory had slaves, that's for sure, but Congress was trying its best to maintain an absolute balance. Until a new 'slave' state could be admitted, there was no hope for Oregon. Nevertheless, in November 1857, 10,000 Oregon voters approved a measure *for* statehood and *against* slavery.

Finally, in 1859, Congress approved the statehood bill and President Buchanan signed it into law. Oregon became the 33rd state.

By that time lumber had been big business in Oregon for over 30 years. It all started in 1825, when the first sawmill was established at Fort Vancouver and the Hudson's Bay Company ordered that trade in timber be given precedence over fur. From that day on, the tall ships of the Pacific Northwest began shuttling trees or cut lumber up and down the coast and off to distant points, including Hawaii and the East Coast. By 1849 more than one million board feet of Douglas fir lumber was shipped from Oregon to San Francisco. And by the time of statehood in 1859, lumbering was the most important industry in Oregon.

It never occurred to anyone that there wouldn't always be an unlimited supply of trees. By 1906 logs were being shipped to sixty-seven countries. They chopped and cut in huge swaths and burned the stumps left behind.

At first they chopped the trees one at a time in teams of two. They would drive a wedge into the trunk about 5 feet above the ground to stand on. Then, using a huge, cross-cut saw, one man on either side of the tree, they would saw away. The cry of "t-i-m-b-e-r" would eventually puncture the air as everyone scrambled to avoid the falling tree.

Logs were skidded down the hillsides to rivers, where they were lashed together to form rafts. The log rafts acted as way stations for the logs until they were transported down the river to waiting ships.

Then the logging machines came to Oregon. Hitched to engines, they cut trees, shaved off bark and sawed trees into lumber in a tenth the time it took mere men. And the machinery made lumbering big business indeed. Oregon men made millions in lumber. And they helped make Oregon the special place we know today. Take Simon Benson, for example. Benson started as a small-time logger and farmer in St. Helens, Oregon. Impoverished for many years, he nevertheless managed to buy timber land. Eventually, he owned 45,000 acres. With discarded donkey engines, he constructed a Rube Goldberg locomotive, laid his own tracks and sent his logs to the coast on his own railroad. That saved him considerable time and money.

Spurred on by the success of his railroad, he decided to ship his logs to the prosperous buyers in Southern California. He knew railroad rates were exorbitant to California and the cost of building his own railroad that far was out of the question. So, he built log rafts instead. His rafts were as much as 835 feet long and could carry up to 4.5 million feet of logs. He towed them the 1,100 miles to San Diego, where an eager market grabbed them up.

In 1910 Benson sold all his timber holdings and launched on a new career. Developer might be a good title. In 1913 he opened the glamorous new Benson Hotel that still bears his name. It's a grand building modeled after the Blackstone Hotel in Chicago and cost Benson a cool $1 million. It's still the grand dame of Portland hotels.

After that, Benson's great passion became roads. He believed in the automobile, and knew good roads were necessary in a society that would one day be dominated by these new-fangled contraptions.

He especially wanted to see a road built along the Columbia River so Sunday drivers could enjoy the lovely scenery. He purchased Multnomah and Wahkeena Falls so they could be turned into public parks for all to enjoy. He championed a state bond issue that was passed to provide the first match for a new federal highway grant, and worked for passage of the first gasoline tax in the nation that was earmarked for highway construction and maintenance. The scenic Columbia River Highway was opened in 1915 and Benson was named chairman of the Oregon State Highway Commission in 1917. Benson once said:

"Do you know why I kept up such an agitation for better roads? It was because we kept talking about getting back to the land, and what it really meant was 'getting back to the mud.' How could we expect to get more producers upon the land and imprison men each winter on their farms with impassable roads? No wonder the children didn't want to stay on the farms."

Oregon continues to enjoy some of the finest roads in the United States. From the Columbia River Highway to scenic U.S. 101 that winds its way along the treacherous, but awesomely beautiful, Oregon coast, the highways give us access to the wonder and beauty of nature. Private nature trails, backwoods roads and ambitious hiking trails lead us away from the rushing traffic to the quiet and peace of the forests and beaches beyond. Thank you, Simon Benson.

And then there was Henry L. Pittock. Pittock was merely 18 when he arrived in Portland in 1853. He immediately started to work on *The Morning Oregonian* and in seven years he was the owner. He remained in control for almost 75 years. But Pittock didn't confine his interests to the newspaper by any means. He jumped in and out of real estate, banking, timber and paper production.

Perhaps the most visible reminder of the success and wealth of Pittock, however, is the Pittock Mansion, commanding a 180 degree view of the Portland area. For 50 years Pittock and his family had lived in a six room cottage in downtown Portland. When he moved at age 79 to his magnificent, new, 22 room mansion on 46 landscaped acres, it was a dramatic example of upward mobility in Portland.

The Pittock Mansion is now one of Portland's major tourist attractions. It's a fantastic French Renaissance chateau, with an interior that includes marble fireplaces, Tiffany wall glaze, a Turkish smoking room, elegant plasterwork and cast bronze. Remarkable modern additions include room-to-room telephones, a central vacuum-cleaning system and an elevator to all floors. He even put in a toe-testing spigot for testing the water temperature before entering the shower.

The Frank family were certainly a fortunate addition to Portland, too. Sigmund Frank was born in Bechtheim, Germany, and arrived in Portland in 1872. He came to work for

Aaron Meier, whom he had met in San Francisco. Meier had a small general store down on S.W. Front Street.

With Frank's help the store prospered, and soon they were ready to expand. They formed the partnership of Meier and Frank in 1874. In 1885 Sigmund Frank married Aaron Meier's daughter, Fanny, which solidified the business and family partnerships.

When Meier died in 1889, Frank became president of the store and continued in that capacity for 21 years. Under Frank's leadership, the store grew in stature and prestige until it enjoyed one of the finest reputations on the West Coast.

Sigmund Frank made another contribution that endeared him to Portland. Actually trained as a violinist in Germany before coming to the United States, he longed for the music of his youth. His wife Fanny was a pianist and violinist herself. He was constantly organizing musical evenings and eventually started the Portland Symphony Orchestra. He even performed as principal violinist for several years.

On Sigmund's death in 1910, the presidency of Meier and Frank fell to Meier's eldest son, Abraham. Julius, the youngest Meier son, became vice president.

Julius was incredibly energetic and worked as hard at the store as he did at everything else. It was once said of him, "Julius Meier's genius, resourcefulness and untiring energy have been the mainspring in making that great department store the huge and successful business it is today." Yet Julius found time for civic duties as well. He built hotels in Eugene and Vancouver, resorts on the Oregon Coast and in the mountains; he became a principal in a bank and, as a crowning achievement, became Governor of Oregon in 1931.

Yet, when the bank fell on hard times during the depression of 1933, it was Julius's nephew, Sigmund's son Aaron Frank, who saved the bank and uncle Julius's reputation. It was Frank who loaned the bank enough money to keep it in business until he could negotiate a sale to the First National Bank. That was only the beginning of a career that was as distinguished as any in Portland's history.

In 1933, Frank assumed the presidency of the Meier and Frank store. His older brother, Lloyd, was no longer affiliated with the business. Lloyd's legacy is the magnificent family home he built on Palatine Hill in Dunthorpe in the 1920s. It's currently part of the campus of Lewis and Clark College.

It was Aaron on the Frank side who assumed civic duties, as well as professional ones. When Earl Riley was Mayor in the

1940s, there was seldom a matter that he didn't discuss with Frank before taking action. The family store was sold in 1965.

Now, it's Aaron's son Gerry who is continuing to carry the civic standard. A multi-talented man, Gerry has been Senator Mark Hatfield's Administrative Assistant for 19 years. But just like his father, he has unbounded energy. He's also found time to write a guide to New York City that's a best seller and to establish a bakery in Salem that sells the most delicious treats imaginable – especially the chocolate ones.

And then there was Henry Villard. Not actually an Oregonian, he contributed more to Oregon's development than almost anyone.

Villard arrived in New York from Germany in 1853. In his own words, he described his arrival: "I was utterly destitute of money, had but a limited supply of wearing apparel and that not suited to the approaching cold season, and I literally did not know a single person in New York or elsewhere in the Eastern States to whom I could apply for help and counsel. To crown all, I could not speak a word of English." He was eighteen years old.

Twenty years later Villard, who had distinguished himself in the fields of teaching and journalism in his adopted land, found himself plunging into a brand new enterprise. Out of a chance meeting in Germany in 1872, Villard agreed to represent the stockholders of the Oregon and California Railroad Company.

He visited Oregon in 1874 and was hooked. He immediately saw the potential for profit in railroading and soon made himself president of the new company he called the Oregon Railway and Navigation Company. By 1883, Villard had spent $20,000,000 building over five hundred miles of roadbed and could smile in the knowledge that his line was the most profitable in the United States.

Villard had his worries, though. Word had it the Northern Pacific was planning to terminate its cross-country line in Tacoma, Washington. That would undermine Villard's enterprise. He was committed to Portland. On the other hand, he was also committed to the old adage that "If you can't beat them, join them." So, he devised an alternative scheme. He quietly started buying up Northern Pacific stock. But he needed more money. His credit and word were so good that when he appealed to his Wall Street friends to invest in a project – without revealing what the project was – he was able to raise $8,000,000. They all called it Villard's 'Blind Pool.'

By 1881, he was president of the Northern Pacific Railroad

Company and he made Portland his western terminus, connecting it with all his other feeder lines already in place.

One thing you could say for Villard – he had impeccable taste. He was especially fond of the leading U.S. architectural firm of McKim, Mead and White. He had had them build him a magnificent house on Madison Avenue in New York. Now he commissioned them to build a series of railroad stations across the nation. What a contribution to our architectural heritage!

In Portland, he decided it would be great if they designed a hotel for his railway passengers. The $1,000,000 Portland Hotel opened in 1890 and was wonderfully magnificent, with the palm-filled dining room, and its exterior decorated with corner towers, awnings and flowers everywhere. It remained in operation for many years and was finally purchased by the Meier and Frank Company in 1944. In 1952 it was demolished.

Yes, by the turn of the century, thanks to these ambitious entrepreneurs, Portland was quite an elegant city. In 1888 Olin Levi Warner finished his magnificent and elaborate masterpiece, the Skidmore fountain, to quench the thirst of 'men, horses and dogs.' It was, and is, one of the finest public monuments in any city.

It was about this same time that residential streets with wide, grassy parks, set with benches and planted with elm trees were laid out, creating Portland's unique 'Park Blocks' – still one of the most pleasant places to promenade in any city.

So, there they are, Oregonians as varied as their professions. What makes them different? Well, they're just Oregonians, you know. Perhaps Governor Tom McCall, beloved by Oregon folks because he was such an Oregonian himself, said it best:

"Your average Oregonian... He is a conservative progressive; that is, he is not opposed to innovation, but he wants to have an idea of where it leads before he approves of starting out. He's a good neighbor and kind to man and beast alike. He is independent politically, and his vote is unpredictable, except that he votes for the candidate a lot more often than mere party label."

Or, maybe it was John Richard Nokes, longtime editor of the *Oregonian*, who knew best: "An Oregonian is a peculiar critter. He is wet on the west side and dry on the east; he is the sand of the beach and snow of the mountains. He is verdant valleys and parched deserts. He came by covered wagon and train and automobile and jet plane. He came from the midwest and the south; from eastern seaboard and Latin America; from Hollywood and from China. He came from farms and ghettoes; from tribes before the white man and from jungles of Africa. He came from the countries of Europe. He is an intellectual and a farmer; a boss and a worker. He is religious and irreligious. He is a conservative and a liberal. Most of all he's a cantankerous independent. A motto from America's Revolutionary War suits him well; 'Don't Tread on Me!'"

Facing page: sunset over Harris Beach State Park.

Above and top left: Brookings Harbor, and (left) Gold Beach marina. Top and facing page: the botanical gardens in Shore Acres State Park, near Coos Bay.

Previous pages: sandy beaches and rocky shorelines combine to form some of Oregon's finest coastal scenery in Cape Sebastian State Park (left) and Harris Beach State Park (right and facing page). Above: visitors watch for sea lions from the viewing area at Sea Lion Point, north of Florence.

Previous pages: spectacular views of Oregon's rugged coastline, looking north from Cape Sebastian Park (right) and within Samuel H. Boardman State Park (left and facing page). Above: a secluded beach near Pistol River, and (overleaf) large rocks dominating the seashore in Harris Beach State Park.

The chalk cliffs of Cape Blanco State Park (above) contrast with the wind-rippled sands of Umpqua Lighthouse State Park (facing page), part of the Oregon Dunes National Recreation Area. Overleaf: (left) the sandstone coast of Shore Acres State Park, and (right) cormorants near Heceta Head.

Top left and top: Honeyman Memorial State Park, part of the Oregon Dunes National Recreation Area (these pages), which comprises 42 miles of protected coastline. Overleaf: (left) the view south along Heceta Beach towards Florence, and (right) Yaquina Head Lighthouse.

Previous pages: (left) Steller sea lions basking near the famous Sea Lion Caves, within sight of Heceta Head Lighthouse (right). Oregon and Washington are linked by a bridge (bottom right and facing page) that spans the Columbia River in Astoria, on the busy northern Oregon coast. Having marked the mouth of the Columbia River for over 50 years, the restored lightship *Columbia* (far right) now lies idle in retirement. Further south, the waters near Depoe Bay (below) yield rich pickings for commercial and sports fishermen. Yaquina Bay Bridge (right and overleaf right) is a familiar landmark in Newport, the largest port on the central Oregon coast. Overleaf left: Cannon Beach stretching away south from Ecola State Park.

Previous pages: weathered pines above the shore south of Cannon Beach. Cannon Beach (these pages and overleaf) occupies a 7-mile-long stretch of coastline between Tillamook Head and Arch Cape in northern Oregon and was named for a cannon reputedly washed ashore in 1846. In recent years the town of Cannon Beach has become a major center for the arts.

Forested headlands and offshore rocks (facing page) south of Ecola State Park contrast with the wide sweep of Nehalem Bay (above) seen from Oswald West State Park. Overleaf: dramatic views of Oregon's coastline, south of Cannon Beach (left), and in Harris Beach State Park (right).

Above: Tolovana Beach Wayside, near Cannon Beach (overleaf left), and
(facing page) a curve of white beach in Oswald West State Park. Further south
lies Netarts Bay (overleaf right), between Cape Meares and Cape Lookout.

Latourell Falls (above), Wahkeena Falls (facing page left) and Multnomah Falls (facing page right) all cascade down the rocky walls of the Columbia River Gorge (overleaf left), an area of spectacular natural beauty. Top left: Cannon Beach, and (left) dunes on Cape Kiwanda. Overleaf right: Saddle Mountain, near Necanicum.

Top: flowers in Washington Park, and (above) tramlines on 1st Avenue, Portland (these pages). Overleaf: Portland's colorful skyline seen across the Willamette River.

Situated nearly 1,000 feet above the city in the hills west of the Willamette, magnificent Pittock Mansion (this page) was purchased by the City of Portland in 1964, restored and opened for public viewing. Facing page: a summer evening concert in Washington Park, Portland.

Pioneer Courthouse Square (facing page), in the center of downtown Portland, is a popular exhibition venue. Right: Morrison Street, and (far right) apartment buildings beside Lovejoy Park, both near Portland Center. Below: polar bears at Portland Zoo, one of the oldest zoos in the country, where over 400 exotic and native animals are housed. Bottom right: the 19th-century home of Dr. John McLoughlin, "the father of Oregon," in Oregon City, 12 miles south of Portland. The white, clapboard house has been carefully restored, refurnished and opened as a museum, and contains many of Dr. McLoughlin's personal belongings.

Many visitors are attracted to the beautifully-landscaped International Rose Test Gardens (below and overleaf right), laid out with more than 10,000 rose bushes of hundreds of varieties, and the tranquil Japanese Gardens (remaining pictures and overleaf left), both in Washington Park, Portland. Set within the largest and busiest of Portland's parks, these gardens open onto fine views of the city and distant mountains.

Oregon's capital city, Salem (this page and overleaf), lies south of the city of Portland (facing page). Built in the 1870s, Bush House (top left), the former home of one of Salem's prominent civic leaders, is now maintained as a museum, while at the Mission Mill Museum (left) a number of Salem's historic buildings have been assembled and restored for public viewing. Above: Willson Park, bordering the west side of the Oregon State Capitol, and (left) the bronze State Seal at the entrance to the capitol.

Built in 1893-94 and set in five
acres of carefully-tended grounds,
Deepwood House (this page), Salem,
has been preserved for the public to
enjoy. Oregon's distinctive state
capitol (facing page), also in Salem,
is faced with white Danby Vermont
marble and topped by a statue of the
Oregon Pioneer finished in gold
leaf. Overleaf: (left) Warm Springs
River in the Warm Springs Indian
Reservation, south of Mount Hood,
and (right) the Sahalie Falls.

At 11,235, feet Oregon's highest mountain, Mount Hood (these pages), dominates the Cascade Range (overleaf right) and offers year-round skiing. Left: Timberline Lodge, (top left) Trillium Lake and (overleaf left) Lost Lake, all in Mount Hood National Forest.

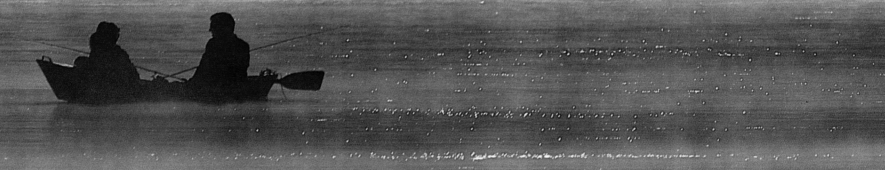

Between Portland and The Dalles, the Columbia River has carved a gorge of spectacular beauty through the Cascade Range (these pages and overleaf). Within the ravine, a still pool in Oneonta Gorge (above) contrasts with the plunging white water of 620-foot-high Multnomah Falls (facing page), the highest waterfall in Oregon, Wahkeena Falls (overleaf left) and Latourell Falls (overleaf right).

Top: harvested fields near Pendleton, and (above) pasture below the Wallowa Mountains. Top right and right: Wallowa Lake, near Joseph, and (facing page) the highway near Stanfield. Overleaf: (left) Mount Hood, and (right) the Scenic Highway beside the Columbia River, seen from Rowena Crest Viewpoint.

rved by the Snake River, 125-mile-long Hells Canyon (previous pages, :ing page: top right and bottom left, above and overleaf) forms a natural undary between Oregon and Idaho. Lined by steep cliffs more than a mile high for nearly 40 miles of its length, it is the deepest river gorge in North America. Facing page: (top left) farm buildings near Oxbow, and (bottom right) Halfway.

Above: Lake Abert in southern Oregon, and (facing page and overleaf left) sunset over open country west of Brothers. Overleaf right: a bridge over the Crooked River in Peter Skene Ogden State Park near Redmond.

Above: the road to Kah-Nee-Ta resort in Warm Springs Indian Reservation, and (facing page) the Crooked River wending its way through Smith Rock State Park. Overleaf: (left) fields near Shaw, and (right) nearby South Falls, one of 14 waterfalls in Silver Falls State Park, 29 miles east of Salem.

Above: 10,497-foot-high Mount Jefferson dominates the skyline above Detroit Lake. Broken Top (facing page) and Todd Lake (overleaf right) lie in Deschutes National Forest, which covers 1,600,460 acres on the eastern slopes of the Cascade Range. Overleaf left: trees line an inviting stretch of open road near Crater Lake in Umpqua National Forest.

Eugene (facing page and overleaf), in the southern Willamette Valley, is the state's second largest city. Home of the University of Oregon (facing page top left), Eugene also offers excellent shopping facilities in, for example, Fifth Street Public Market (top right) and an attractive downtown mall (bottom left). The Hult Center for the Performing Arts (bottom right) is a popular cultural venue. The distinctive Memorial Union building (below) of Oregon State University and Benton County Courthouse (right), built in 1888, can be found in Corvallis, north of Eugene. Far right: a fine Victorian house in Albany, and (bottom right) Jackson Street in Roseburg.

Previous pages: (left) Sunrise Lodge on the slopes of Mount Bachelor (right), some 22 miles west of Bend. Access to the summit is by chairlift, from which can be seen the Three Sisters and Broken Top (above). Mount Bachelor (facing page) attracts skiers of all standards to the Mount Bachelor Ski Area, central Oregon's leading ski resort.

Above and overleaf right: Crater Lake National Park. Facing page: Tillamook
Head, on the northern Oregon coast, enveloped in mist, and (overleaf left)
Broken Top seen from Todd Lake in Deschutes National Forest.

Crater Lake (these pages and overleaf left) lies within a huge volcanic caldera
six miles in diameter and, with a depth of 1,932 feet, is the deepest lake in the
United States. Overleaf right: Crater Lake Lodge.

Above: farm buildings east of the timber town of Roseburg, and (facing page)
the nearby North Umpqua River, in Umpqua National Forest. Overleaf:
Wizard Island rises above the deep blue waters of Crater Lake.